Continents Toge....

Jean Feldman and Holly Karapetkova

Tune: He's Got the Whole World in His Hands

www.rourkeclassroom.com

We've got the whole world in our hands.

We've got the whole world in our hands.

We've got the whole world in our hands.

We've got the whole world in our hands.

We've got **North** and **South America** in our hands.

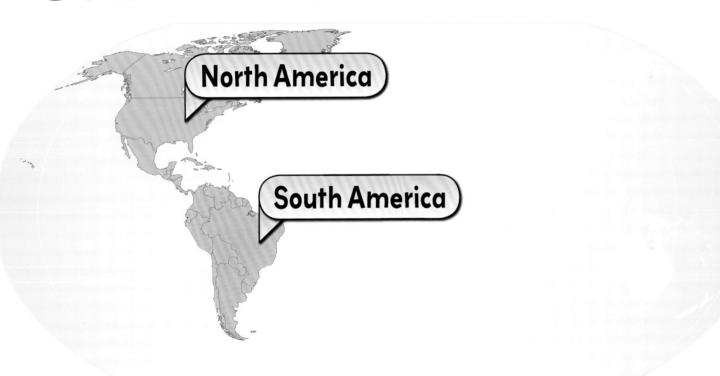

We've got **Europe**, **Asia**, **Africa** in our hands.

We've got **Australia** and **Antarctica** in our hands.

We've got the whole world in our hands.

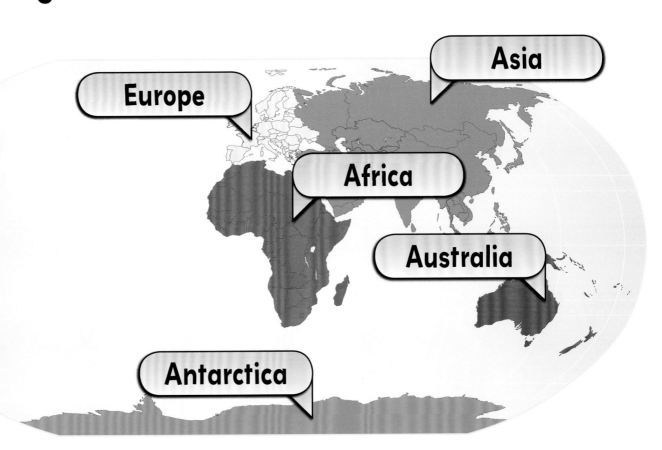

We've got to work together to keep it green.
Protect our planet's lands and seas.

We can all make a difference,
You know what I mean.

We've got to help keep it green.

Come on North and
South America keep it green.

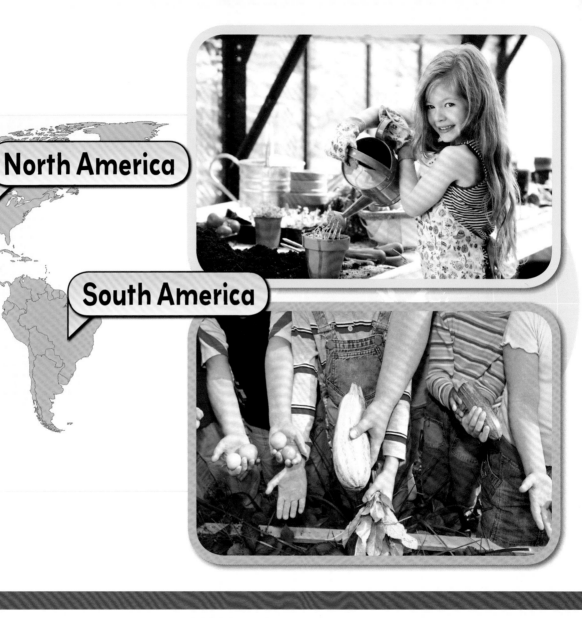

North America

South America

Come on **Europe**, **Asia**, **Africa** keep it green.

Come on **Australia** and **Antarctica** keep it green.

Let's keep our planet clean.

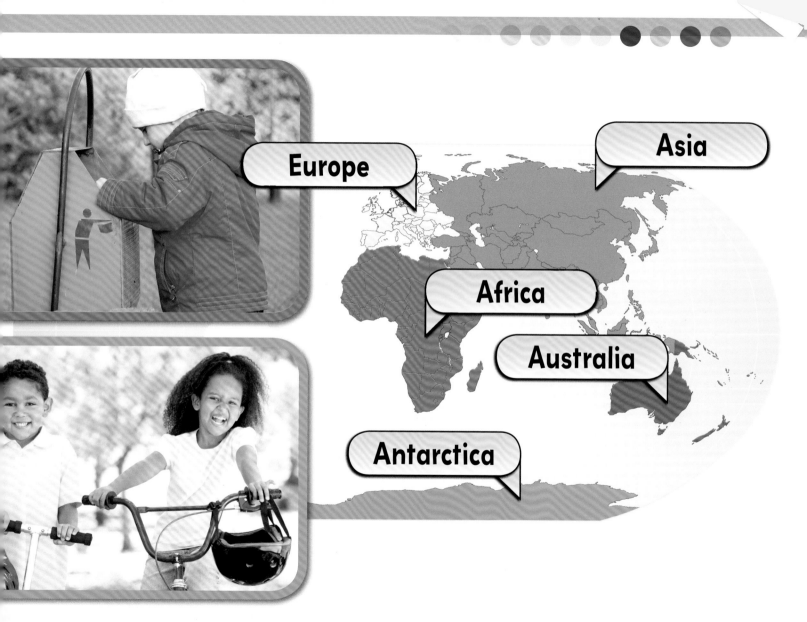

We've got the whole world in our hands.

We've got the whole world in our hands.

We've got the whole world in our hands.

Together we'll keep it GREEN!